# THE RESP BOOK

## *The Complete Guide to Registered Education Savings Plans for Canadians*

D0558342

Mike Holman

Money Smarts Publishing
Toronto, Canada

**Author Online!**

For more RESP and other personal finance and
investment information,
visit Mike Holman's blog at:

**www.moneysmartsblog.com**

ISBN 978-0-9866489-0-8

*The more that you read, the more things you will know.*
*The more that you learn, the more places you'll go.*

**Dr. Seuss**

*Education costs money, but then so does ignorance.*

**Claus Moser**

*Genius without education is like silver in the mine.*

**Benjamin Franklin**

*To my wife and kids,*
*who support everything I do,*
*as long as they can be with me.*

# CONTENTS

# 1
# INTRODUCTION TO RESPs

*Topics covered in this chapter:*

- *Benefits of RESP accounts*
- *Why you should start an RESP account*
- *Why you shouldn't start an RESP account*
- *How much you need to contribute to an RESP*
- *An estimate of future educational costs*
- *RESPs for adults*

# *What is an RESP?*

*RESP* stands for Registered Educational Savings Plan. An RESP is an investment account that can receive extra grants from the government based on the amount contributed. The investments in these accounts enjoy tax-free growth and earnings, meaning more money will be available for future educational costs.

There are many rules, regulations and limits for RESPs, so this book covers the important information that the typical RESP investor needs to know. The basics of investing and how to open an RESP account are also outlined.

RESPs can be opened at most banks, with a financial advisor or even on your own as a self-directed RESP. Scholarship, group or pooled plans are also available, but I don't recommend them because of high costs and restrictive rules.

It's important to know that RESPs are a type of investment account, not a type of investment. You can put the same types of investments in an RESP as a Registered Retirement Savings Plan (RRSP). Guaranteed Investment Certificates (GICs), stocks, bonds, mutual funds, exchanged traded funds (EFTs) and good old cash are all eligible investments for your RESP.

The purpose of having an RESP account is to help save for a child's education. Typically, parents open RESPs for their own children, but you can open an RESP account for any child.

# 6 Reasons to Start an RESP

There are many reasons why you should start an RESP. Saving for your child's education will likely improve the odds that she will participate in post-secondary education by diminishing financial barriers and building a financial nest egg. An RESP account should make it easier on your budget when she is in school.

Here are some of the great things about RESP accounts:

**1 CESG (Canadian Education Savings Grant)**

RESPs can receive extra grants called CESGs from the government based on the amount contributed to the account. CESGs are worth 20% of each dollar you contribute and are basically free money. The CESG is the single biggest reason why an RESP account is usually far superior to any other type of savings or investment account for educational saving purposes.

**2 Tax-free compounding**

All interest payments, dividends and capital gains earned inside an RESP account are not taxable. This means you get to keep all of the money earned, increasing the amount of money available for your child's education. If you start the RESP account when your child is young, there will be many years for that investment to grow tax-free.

**3 Dedicated savings account**

It is a good idea to have a separate savings account for a major financial goal like post-secondary education. If this money were mixed in with other types of savings, it would be easier to spend it on items other than education.

5

**4 Reduce your liabilities when your child is at school**

Some parents find themselves in the situation where their child is attending college or university, and they end up having to funnel a large amount of their budget to pay for the schooling. With a fully funded RESP, there should be little or no financial demands on the parents once the child starts post-secondary education.

**5 Reduce student loans for your child**

One alternative to parents paying for a large amount of the education is for the child to apply for student loans. While this strategy isn't the worst thing in the world, it would be ideal for the student to avoid any debt while in school.

**6 Reduce your child's need to work during the school year**

I'm a big fan of students working during the summer, but I don't think they should have to work during the school year. Students should be free to work hard in their studies while also participating in sports or social activities.

# 6 Reasons Not to Start an RESP

RESPs are not for everyone. If you are not in a position to make contributions to an RESP, you should wait before opening one.

Here are some reasons to avoid opening an RESP account:

## 1 You need to get your finances in order

If you have excessive debts or spend more than you make, you should wait to open an RESP. You might end up cashing in the RESP to pay your bills, defeating the purpose of setting up the RESP in the first place. It is important to get control of your finances and fix the here-and-now before worrying about the future.

## 2 Your retirement savings are inadequate

There is no exact amount of retirement savings you should have at any given age, but if you are working full time and don't have any retirement savings, you are not saving enough. The older you are and the less you've saved, the more you should worry about saving for your retirement rather than saving for your child's education. Your child can borrow to pay for her education, but you can't borrow for your retirement.

## 3 No extra money in your budget

If your finances are in good order but you don't have any extra money, you obviously can't make RESP contributions. In this case, you might want to consider trimming your budget in order to free up some money for RESP contributions. Another idea is to look at ways to make extra income so that you can save for your child's education.

7

A great book for money-saving ideas is <u>397 Ways to Save Money</u> by Kerry Taylor.

**4 Pay-as-they-go educational funding strategy**

One common strategy for parents is to pay down all their debts before the child starts school. Once the child starts post-secondary education, there should be lots of extra cash in the budget to pay for education bills. The drawback of this plan is that you don't get any of the juicy RESP grant money.

**5 You want your child to pay for part or all of the education**

It is reasonable to ask your child to pay for part of her education. The drawback of this plan is that she might end up not going to school or dropping out if the financial burden is too onerous. If the student works part-time during the school year, her grades could be affected. Alternatively, she might graduate with large student debts.

**6 Your children are too old or ineligible for RESP grants**

The last year your child can receive a grant in her RESP is the year she turns 17. However, children who are 16 and 17 are only eligible for grants if they meet certain eligibility requirements, which are outlined in Chapter 3: RESP Contributions and Grants. Creating an RESP for a child who is ineligible for the RESP grants has very limited benefits and is likely not worthwhile.

# How much should you contribute to an RESP?

The amount you contribute to an RESP is highly dependent on your personal financial circumstances. Here are some things to consider when deciding on your contribution plan.

**What are your goals?**

Do you want to pay for all of your child's educational costs? Half of them? The more money you want to have available for post-secondary education, the higher the contributions will have to be and the sooner you'll need to start the RESP account.

**How many years until they go to school?**

If you wait until your children are older to start an RESP account, there will be less time for contributions and investment growth. This means that larger contributions will be required, compared to someone who starts the RESP when the children are young.

**How much can you afford?**

In order to get the maximum annual RESP grant of $500, you must contribute $2,500 per year or $208.33 per month to the RESP account. The reality is that many people might not be able to spare this much from their budget. My philosophy is that something is infinitely better than nothing, so even if you can only handle $50 per month, you should do it. If your finances improve in the future, you can always increase the monthly contribution. Even if you only contribute $50 per month from when the child is young, that will still add up to a substantial amount by the time the child goes to school.

9

**Will the student be living at home while attending post-secondary school?**

In my mind, this is one of the two biggest uncertainties regarding post-secondary education costs (the other being whether the child will attend post-secondary school at all). The problem is that the amount of money required for a student to attend school out of town is roughly twice the amount necessary if they live at home. By the time you find out where the child will be going to school, it will be too late to adjust your RESP contribution strategy.

One solution is to save just enough for the student to live at home and go to school. If he wants to go to school in a different city, he can pay the extra costs himself. This plan only works if there are schooling options in your city.

My plan is to make the maximum contributions for my children and just keep the excess amounts for myself if they end up going to school in our city. If they are living at home, my children probably won't need the entire RESP savings.

Other options for utilizing excess contributions include:
- Give them to the child after graduation to help get her started.
- Use them for further education, such as a Master's degree.
- Contribute them to another RESP for a younger sibling.

*Read more information on withdrawing contribution amounts in Chapter 4: RESP Withdrawal Rules When Child Attends Post-Secondary Education.*

**Will you be working or retired when your children go to school?**

For younger parents, there is a pretty good chance that they will be working during the child's school years. If their RESP account savings are insufficient, younger parents can probably make up the difference from their income -- which reduces the pressure of making large RESP contributions.

For older parents like myself, there is a reasonable chance that they won't be working during the child's post-secondary school years. If you will be retired when your child is attending post-secondary education, your options will be limited if the RESP account does not contain enough money. In this case, it is more important to make sufficient RESP contributions during your working years.

10

# Future post-secondary educational costs

Every once in a while, a financial institution does a study on future educational costs and releases it to the media. This is done to encourage parents to contribute more money to their RESP accounts and to help those financial companies make more money.

I usually find these studies quite depressing because they always foresee incredibly large future educational costs. You will often see estimates well in excess of $130,000 for a complete post-secondary education.

For several reasons, I decided to ignore these reports and just come up with my own estimate. My estimate might not be perfectly accurate, but I doubt it is any less accurate than the scare reports issued by financial companies.

## 7 Problems with educational cost estimates in media reports

### 1 Conflict of interest

Any company that offers RESP accounts has a vested interest in publishing studies that promote RESP sales. By making more aggressive assumptions about future costs, a company can easily inflate future educational cost estimates.

### 2 Inflation

The direct costs of education, such as tuition, have been rising at rates significantly higher than inflation. Most studies assume that this trend will continue indefinitely, which may or may not actually happen.

### 3 Living costs

Items like food, shelter and other living costs are difficult to estimate and are quite controllable by the student. I suspect these studies estimate these costs on the high end.

### 4 RESP will pay 100% of educational costs

These studies assume that the RESP account is the sole source of funds to pay for your child's education. The reality is that your child may have other sources of income to pay for school.

Most students work in the summer or on co-op work terms and can help pay for some of their educational costs. Some students will work during the school year as well. Lastly, unless parents are in a dire financial situation, they should be able to throw in a bit of cash for any shortfalls as they arise. And of course student loans, grants and scholarships might be a possibility as well.

### 5 Will the child be living at home?

Most future educational cost studies I've seen assume the child will not be living at home – which of course adds greatly to the cost. This assumption ignores the huge cost reduction that is possible if the child lives at home during post-secondary schooling.

### 6 Future dollars

Most of these studies use future dollars, which are larger because of the effects of inflation. Most of your RESP contributions and earnings will be in future dollars as well.

### 7 They project 17 years into the future

In order to maximize the *shock* effect of the estimates, the timeline of the studies is usually 17 years, which adds to the future cost because of inflation. This estimate would be relevant for a brand new parent whose child won't be going to school for 17 years, but for parents with children who are not newborns, the estimate is too high.

**Let's work through a scenario**

One estimate for current post-secondary educational costs is $77,132 for a student going to school out of town and $51,763 if the student lives at home.[1]

That may sound like a lot of money, but let's work through the numbers to find out how this amount can be paid without relying 100% on the RESP account. The dollar amounts are all in today's dollars for easier comparison. I'm assuming the RESP contributions start in the child's first year.

**Scenario 1: Student does not live with parents**

The total amount needed for educational costs in 2010 dollars is $77,132.

Let's assume the student works during the summers, saving $1,000 for her first year and $2,000 for the second, third and fourth years. The total saved from her summer jobs is $7,000. With the extra savings, the student's total education costs are now $70,132.

Her parents will pay $2,400 per year ($200 per month) from their regular budget for all four years of schooling. Their total contribution of $9,600 brings the student's total costs down to $60,532.

Assuming withdrawals from the RESP account will fund the remaining shortfall, let's tally how much should be contributed each month:

If you assume a real rate of return[2] of 4%, you will need to **contribute $163.83 per month** in order to reach this goal. This results in an annual contribution of $1,966, which is well short of the maximum $2,500. The RESP grant would be paid on top of that contribution amount.

**Scenario 2: Student lives with parents**

Total amount of money needed in 2009 dollars is $51,763.

In this scenario as well, we will assume that the student can save $7,000 over the four years and that the parents will chip in $9,600, leaving us with a shortfall of $35,163.

1   http://www.td.com/economics/special/ca1009_education.pdf
2   Real rate of return is the increase in value of your investments, minus inflation.

13

Assuming a real rate of return of 4%, the monthly RESP contribution amount necessary to make up this shortfall is only **$95.17 per month**! This works out to an annual contribution of $1,142 -- which is less than half of the maximum contribution amount.

These scenarios show that you don't have to contribute the maximum amount every year in order to ensure that your child has enough money for post-secondary education.

As for the problem of not knowing if your child will be living at home, you can contribute enough to pay for the child living away from home, and then keep the contributions for yourself if she ends up living at home.

# RESPs for adults are a waste of time

RESPs are not just for kids. You are allowed to open an individual RESP for yourself and make contributions that can be withdrawn for educational purposes.

The RESP rules for adults are similar to the rules for children except for that there are no government grants available, greatly reducing the attractiveness of this strategy.

The main drawback of the RESP account is the penalty on earnings (20% tax in addition to income tax) if the beneficiary doesn't go to school. For a younger person, the free government grant makes the risk worthwhile. In my opinion, this risk is not worthwhile for an adult who can't qualify for the RESP grant.

Adults who want to save for their own education should consider using the new Tax Free Savings Account (TFSA). This account is tax-sheltered and doesn't have any withdrawal penalties.

## Chapter 1 Summary

RESPs are intended to help with a child's post-secondary educational costs. Penalties will be applied if the money is used for other purposes.

RESP accounts are tax-sheltered accounts that are eligible for government grant money based on contributions. The grants are worth 20% of any eligible contributions.

RESP accounts can be opened with most financial institutions and can contain a wide variety of investments, from GICs to individual stocks.

Educational costs can vary between programs. If a student lives at home, his costs will be much cheaper than if he were living on his own.

RESPs can be used for adults, but the TFSA is a better choice for this purpose.

# 2
# RESP ACCOUNT RULES

*Topics covered in this chapter:*

- *Eligibility for RESP grants*
- *Individual vs. family plan accounts*
- *RESP account requirements*
- *Multiple RESP accounts*
- *RESP account taxation*

When you open an RESP account, there are two important terms to know:

**Subscriber** – The person who opens the RESP account and makes the contributions. Accounts can also be opened with two subscribers. Such accounts are known as **joint** accounts. The subscriber(s) make contributions to the account and are responsible for investment decisions as well as managing withdrawals.

**Beneficiary** - The person (usually a child) who is named as the beneficiary of the account and is eligible to receive money from the RESP account if used for educational purposes.

**Eligibility requirements for receiving RESP grants**

In order for a beneficiary to be eligible to receive RESP grants from the government, the following conditions must be met:

- Subscriber must have a valid Social Insurance Number (SIN)
- Beneficiary must have a valid SIN
- Beneficiary must be a Canadian resident
- Beneficiary must be 17 years of age or less at the end of the calendar year when the contribution is made -- in other words, the year in which the child turns 17 is the last year they can receive RESP grants

**Ownership of the funds in the RESP account**

The subscriber is always the **owner** of all the funds in an RESP. The money never legally belongs to the beneficiary until it is paid out to her. A person can open an RESP account and later decide to not give any of the money to the beneficiary. This is possible because the money belongs to the subscriber.

**Criteria for opening an RESP account**

- Subscriber must be a person, not a corporation
- Subscriber and beneficiaries must have a valid SIN
- Joint subscribers must be spouses as defined by the *Income Tax Act*
- Maximum two subscribers per plan

There are two types of RESP accounts.

**Individual RESP accounts**

The term *individual* means that there can only be one beneficiary for this type of account.

This type of account can be opened by a person who is not related to the beneficiary. You can even open an RESP account for yourself.

**Family RESP accounts**

Family plans can have one or more beneficiaries. The beneficiaries must be connected to the subscriber by blood or adoption. This includes children, grandchildren or siblings of the subscriber -- either by blood, adoption or marriage. The beneficiaries must be under 21 years old when named. Beneficiaries can be removed or added anytime during the life of the plan.

There are no age limits for family plan beneficiaries; however, CESGs and other grants can only be earned by beneficiaries up to the end of the year in which they turn 17 years old. The beneficiary on the account can be replaced by another child, but if the new beneficiary is not blood-related to the subscriber, any CESGs in the account have to be repaid.

Here are some options for RESP accounts:

- Parents with one child can open an individual account
- Parents with more than one child can open a family plan account
- Parents with one child can open a family plan RESP to allow for future expansion

20

- Parents with one child and an individual RESP account can transfer the funds into a family plan later on if more kids are born
- Parents with more than one child can open an individual account for each child

If you want to open an RESP account for someone who is not your child or grandchild, you must open a separate individual RESP account for each beneficiary you wish to contribute to. You will need the child's SIN to do this. There is no limit to the number of RESP accounts that a person can open. There is also no limit to the number of RESP accounts that list the same beneficiary.

**Should you choose the Family or Individual Plan?**

If you have one child, opening an individual RESP account is the obvious choice. For multiple-child families, it may appear at first glance that family accounts are more flexible than individual accounts. In fact, the two accounts are similar because the rules allow you to transfer money between any type of account. If one of your children does not go to school, it will not matter whether you have your children in a family account or individual accounts since you can transfer RESP funds to other siblings.

Family plans are slightly better if you have more than one child because having one account will help you save on account fees and also might simplify the paperwork.

The bottom line is that it doesn't really matter, so pick the option that results in the lowest account fees and is the most convenient option for you.

**How to handle multiple RESP accounts and subscribers**

When setting up an RESP for a child, it is important to communicate with other relatives and friends who might have also opened an RESP for the same beneficiary. The government will add up all the contributions attributed to each beneficiary in order to enforce the various limits and maximum amounts. This applies to any RESP account opened for a beneficiary – it doesn't matter if they were opened in different financial institutions by different subscribers.

This issue was more important when there was an annual maximum for RESP contributions; however, there is still the $50,000 lifetime contribution to consider as well as maximum annual grant amounts.

If the annual grant-eligible contribution amounts are exceeded, the excess contributions won't be eligible for any grants. If the lifetime contribution limit is exceeded, the extra contributions will be taxed at a rate of 1% per month.

You might be wondering why someone would open an RESP for a relative rather than give the money to the parents to open an RESP. If that parent is not as financially sound as you or perhaps not trusted, you might not want to give him the money for fear that he won't set up the RESP or that he will withdraw the money before the child goes to school. Also, if the child doesn't go to school, the money goes back to the subscriber, so setting up the RESP yourself will ensure that you get your money back.

**Be careful if other people are opening RESP accounts for your children**

If other people want to set up RESPs for your children, keep in mind that they will be the owners of that money until they decide to give it to your children for educational purposes. There could be a long time interval between a friend or relative setting up the RESP and the child going to school. A lot can happen during that time - maybe you won't stay in touch with that person, maybe they will decide to not give the money to your child when they go to school. Perhaps they will die or run into financial difficulty.

I certainly wouldn't go as far as to suggest that you turn down all offers to help, but it might be worthwhile to consider the likelihood that you will be able to get the money from the person offering to set up an RESP for your child. Every child is only eligible for $7,200 of RESP grants in their lifetime. So, if a generous relative is maxing out an RESP for your child but goes bankrupt just before your child starts post-secondary education, she might not be able to give your child the RESP money, and you might be out of luck.

22

**TIP:** If you are a parent and have friends or relatives who want to help out with your child's education - try to get them to contribute to your RESP account. If they contribute to an RESP account where they are the subscriber, you have no control or claim over those funds.

**Taxation within an RESP account**

RESP accounts are tax-sheltered, meaning there are no taxes due on any income earned within the account from grants, dividends or interest payments. Capital gains, which occur when your investments go up in value, are also not taxable.
Contributions to RESP accounts are **not tax-deductible**.

**Estate planning for RESP accounts**

**RESP accounts belong to the subscriber and not to the beneficiaries.**

If the subscriber dies, the account becomes part of the estate. The problem is, if the subscriber's will dictates that the estate be divided between various parties, the RESP might have to be collapsed and the net proceeds divided up. This probably wasn't the intention of the deceased subscriber, but that is what will happen unless the beneficiaries of the estate agree to keep the RESP account intact.

It is important to include a subscriber successor in your will so that the RESP can be used for its intended purpose. If other people have RESP accounts set up for your children, make sure they have indicated in their will that you or someone trustworthy will be the successor subscriber if they die.

23

## Chapter 2 Summary

The **subscriber** is the person who opens the RESP account. This person owns the funds in the RESP account.

The **beneficiary** is the person who receives payments from the RESP as a student.

Individual RESP accounts have one beneficiary. Family RESP accounts have one or more beneficiaries.

More than one RESP account can be opened for the same beneficiary. However, care must be taken to ensure that contribution and grant limits are not exceeded.

Individual RESP accounts can be set up by anyone, even if they are not related to the beneficiary. Be aware that someone who sets up an RESP for your child does not have to give the child any of the money, at any time.

RESP accounts are tax-sheltered. This means that no taxes will be owed on any earnings inside the RESP account.

RESP accounts need to be mentioned in the subscriber's will. Otherwise, the account will go to the estate upon their death.

# 3

# RESP CONTRIBUTIONS AND GRANTS

*Topics covered in this chapter:*

- *Contribution limits*
- *RESP grant limits and amounts*
- *Contribution room carryover rules*
- *Contribution options*
- *Family plan grant allocations*
- *Grant rules for 16- and 17-year-olds*

One of the main benefits of Canada's RESP program is the federal Canadian Educational Savings Grant (CESG). This grant is 20% of any eligible contributions in an RESP account.

These grants are exciting because they are one of the few examples in life of **free money**.

**Here's how the grant system works.**

Let's say you open an RESP account for your bouncing new baby and contribute $1,000 into the account. Your financial institution will send the account and contribution information to the Canadian government for grant approval. If the grant is approved, the institution receives the grant money and deposits it into your account.

The math:

20% of $1,000 is $200, so you will now have an extra $200 in the account courtesy of the Canadian government. This basically gives you an extra 20% one-time return on your contribution, which is pretty sweet.

The government approval process usually results in a delay of at least 30 days from the time you make the contribution to the time the grant money appears in your account.

Please note that contributions to an RESP are **not tax-deductible** like RRSP contributions. You won't get a tax slip, and you can't deduct RESP contributions from your taxable income.

There are many rules regarding the annual grant limits, so let's get started with the ones you need to know. Once we get through the basic rules, we will explore each rule with a detailed example.

Please note that I will be using the term **contribution room** quite frequently. I am referring to the contribution amount that is eligible for a grant. You can contribute more than the *eligible amount* each year, but the excess amount will not receive any grant money.

**$2,500** - Amount of annual contribution room accrued each year starting in 2007 or the year the child was born (whichever is later). The contribution room continues accruing up to and including the year when the child turns 17 years old. This amount is based on the calendar year and not the birth date.

**$2,000** - Amount of annual contribution room accrued each year starting from the year the child was born or 1998 (whichever is later) up to and including 2006.

**20%** - Amount of grant earned on an eligible contribution. For example: a $1,000 contribution would earn a grant of $200, if that contribution is eligible for a grant. There are additional grants available for lower income families, which are detailed in Chapter 6: Additional Grants for Lower Income Families.

**$500** – Maximum amount of grant a beneficiary is eligible to receive for each calendar year from the year they were born or 1998 (whichever is later) to the year they turn 17 years old. This amount was only $400 for years prior to 2007.

**$7,200** - Lifetime grant limit per beneficiary. If you contribute $2,500 every year, you will hit the maximum grant level in the fifteenth year, and no more grants will be paid to the beneficiary. This limit includes additional grants available to lower income families.

**$50,000** - Lifetime contribution limit per beneficiary. Because there is no annual limit, you could potentially make one single contribution of $50,000 to an RESP if you choose.

**Contribution room carry over.** One of the great things about the RESP is that you can carry over unused contribution room into future years. However, there is a catch: Only one previous year's worth of contributions can be used each year.

For example: If you start an account for your six-year-old child, you can contribute $2,500 (this year's contribution room) plus another $2,500 (a previous year's unused contribution room) for a total of $5,000, to receive a grant of $1,000. You are allowed to contribute more than $5,000 in this scenario, but there will be no grant paid on the amount above $5,000. When calculating contribution room carryover from past years, don't forget that the contribution limit was only $2,000 prior to 2007.

Confused? You should be!

Let's do some examples to clarify exactly how this works.

**Example 1 - Simplest example**

Steve was born in 2010. His parents are broke, but one kindly grandmother decides to open an RESP account for him.

She opened the account in 2010 and has $2,500 of contribution room available. She contributes $1,500 to the account in 2010, so the RESP grant is $300 (20% of $1,500).

In 2011, she contributes $1,200, thereby qualifying for a $240 grant.

**Example 2 - A more complicated example:**

Little Johnny was born in 2006. His parents decide in 2010 to set up an RESP account for him. They want to know how much money they can contribute each year to catch up on all the missed government grants.

Let's add up the current contribution room.

2006 - $2,000 of contribution room

2007 - $2,500 (new rules)

2008 - $2,500

2009 - $2,500

2010 - $2,500

In 2010, the couple has $2,500 of contribution room for the current year plus $9,500 of contribution room from previous years.

Since the rule is that you can only contribute up to $2,500 of previously carried over contribution room each year in addition to the current contribution room, this means they can contribute this year's amount ($2,500) and another $2,500 for a total of $5,000, which gives a grant of 20% or $1,000 for 2010. Since they only used $2,500 of their available $9,500 of carried over contribution room, they now have $7,000 in contribution room to carry over for the future.

In 2011, they can contribute another $5,000 for a $1,000 grant. $4,500 of contribution room is carried forward to the next year.

In 2012, they can contribute another $5,000 for a $1,000 grant.

$2,000 of contribution room is carried forward to the next year.

In 2013, they can contribute only $4,500. $2,500 from the current year plus $2,000 they carried over from the past.

In 2014 and beyond, they can only contribute $2,500 each year and expect to receive the full grant of $500.

Summary of contributions they can make to get all the government grants:

2010 - Contribute $5,000, receive $1,000 grant, $7,000 of unused contribution room

2011 - Contribute $5,000, receive $1,000 grant, $4,500 of unused contribution room

2012 - Contribute $5,000, receive $1,000 grant, $2,000 of unused contribution room

2013 - Contribute $4,500, receive $900 grant, $0 of unused contribution room

2014 and onward – Contribute $2,500, receive $500 grant

**Lifetime grant total of $7,200**

The maximum amount of RESP grants that can be paid to one beneficiary in his lifetime is $7,200. Any further contributions for that beneficiary will not receive any grants.

Make sure you are aware of this rule, since neither the government nor your financial institution will notify you if you go over this limit. The only thing that will happen is that that government will stop paying grants on your contributions. There is nothing wrong with contributing to an RESP without the grant, but most people only contribute to an RESP for the grant money.

**$50,000 lifetime contribution limit and lump sum contribution strategy**

Do the math and you will notice that the total contribution amount necessary to reach the lifetime grant total limit of $7,200 is $36,000. Yet, the lifetime contribution limit is $50,000 per child. Why would someone want to contribute more than $36,000 to an RESP when those contributions won't receive any grant money?

The main reason for doing this is the tax-free status of the RESP account. If someone makes extra contributions to an RESP when the child is young, there are many years of tax-free compounding available. If the alternative for this money is a taxable account, the RESP might be a better choice. Now that the TFSA is available for Canadians, it is probably a better choice if you have TFSA contribution room available.

Most Canadians have a hard time contributing any money to an RESP, so over-contributing isn't a realistic scenario for most. However, if you were to receive a large windfall from an inheritance or other source, over-contributing to an RESP when the child is young can be a viable strategy.

If you are really flush with cash, one possible option is to contribute $50,000 to your child's RESP as soon as you open the account in your child's first year. You will only get $500 of grant money on the first $2,500 of contributions, but then you will have at least 18 years of tax-free compounding. This strategy will beat contributing $2,500 per year if the investment returns are high enough; however, it's not something that most Canadians can consider since most of us don't have $50,000 lying around.

If you exceed the $50,000 lifetime contribution limit, the excess amount will be taxed at 1% per month until the excess contribution is withdrawn.

**Maximum age for contributions and grants**

RESP grants can be paid on contributions for beneficiaries up to the **end of the year** in which they turn 17. After that year, contributions can continue to be made, but no grants will be paid.

**Age limits for individual accounts.** There is no age limit on individual accounts. Someone who is 90 years old could set one up for herself. Individual accounts can stay open for a maximum of 36 years.

**Family accounts age limits.** There is also no age limit on family accounts, but contributions cannot be made for a beneficiary after the year in which he or she turns 31. A person can not be named a beneficiary for a family plan unless he or she is under 21. Family accounts can stay open for a maximum of 36 years.

**RESP accounts have flexible contribution options**

The subscriber of an RESP account has a lot of flexibility with respect to contributions. You need to check with your financial institution to see if there are any minimums to adhere to, but otherwise, you are free to pick your own contribution amounts and frequency. None of these options will affect the amount of grants you will receive in the RESP account.

- You can contribute as little as you want each year. Note that some institutions require a minimum of $50 per contribution.
- You don't need to contribute every year. You can contribute once and then never again, every four years -- whatever you like.
- You can contribute with cheques.
- You can set up automatic electronic withdrawals from your bank account.
- You can contribute once a year, once a month or any other frequency that your financial institution is set up for.

Please note there are special contribution rules for 16- and 17-year-olds. *Please read the section **Special grant rules for 16- and 17-year-olds** later in this chapter for details.*

**RESP family plan contribution allocations**

If you have a family plan with two or more beneficiaries, you need to allocate each contribution between the beneficiaries. For example, you might want to set up all contributions to be divided equally between the account beneficiaries. Or you might have a particular contribution that should be allocated to just one beneficiary. You must set the allocation so the government can track the grants for each child..

When you open an RESP account or add a new beneficiary to an existing account, you can set up the default allocation to split the contributions equally among the children on the account. If you want to make a contribution with a different allocation, you have to indicate this on the purchase order.

**Why would I want to have an unequal allocation?**

One reason for having an unequal allocation might be age difference between your children. If you have a 13-year-old and a 7-year-old, you might want to increase the contributions for the 13-year-old in order to get as much of the government grants as you can since there are not as many contribution years remaining for the older child.

**Why would some contributions have different allocations?**

Sometimes relatives or friends want to give a specific gift to one of your children but not the other. For example: A grandmother wants to contribute $200 for each child on his or her birthday. In this case, you can make the contribution and specify that the contribution is for one child. This means that only the specified child receives the grant on that contribution.

The allocation of contributions is important because of the individual grant limits. If you mean to make contributions to two or more beneficiaries and inadvertently allocate all the contributions to one child, you might find that some of your contributions are not receiving grants because there isn't enough contribution room for one beneficiary.

If you add another child to your family plan, make sure the contribution allocation is updated.

**Contribution years are by calendar year**

One of the more common misconceptions about RESP rules is the idea that contribution time frames involve birthdates or account opening dates. This is not the case; the contribution years always involve calendar years.

For example: If a child is born in December of 2010, the contribution room available for 2010 to get the maximum grant is $2,500. When the new calendar year starts on January 1, 2011, a new year of contribution room is available. The subscriber can contribute another $2,500 and get the full $500 grant for that year. **They don't have to wait until the child's birthday.**

The date the account is opened is not relevant with respect to contribution room. If you wait until your daughter is five years old before starting an RESP account, she will still have all of the contribution room available for previous years starting from the year she was born.

### Don't wait too long to open an RESP account

Because of the $1,000 grant limit payable each year, you can only catch up on one year of previously missed contributions each year. This means if you wait too long, you won't be able to get all the $7,200 of grant money.

If your goal is to get the maximum grant money available, you have to make a contribution by the year in which the beneficiary turns 10 at the latest. If you contribute $1,000 to the account in the year in which the child turns 10, and $5,000 per year up to and including the year that she turns 17, the maximum grant amount of $7,200 will be reached. In that case, the total amount of contributions will be $36,000 and the total grants paid will be the maximum of $7,200. If you wait until after the year she turns 10, you will never be able to reach the maximum grant payout.

### Special grant rules for 16- and 17-year-olds

There are special grant eligibility restrictions for 16- and 17-year-olds. These rules apply to the calendar years in which they turn 16 or 17, not the actual age of the child.

RESP contributions made for beneficiaries aged 16 and 17 are eligible for a grant only if at least one of the following conditions is met:

- At least $2,000 must have been contributed to, and not withdrawn from, an RESP for the beneficiary before the end of the calendar year the beneficiary turned 15.

34

- At least $100 must have been contributed to, and not withdrawn from, an RESP for the beneficiary in each of any four years before the end of the calendar year in which the beneficiary turned 15.

**What this means**

If you open a child's first RESP in the year he turns 16 or 17 years of age, no grants will be paid. It is too late.

For a child to be eligible for RESP grants in the year she turns 16 or 17, either of the following conditions must be met:

1) A total of $2,000 must be contributed toward the child's RESP by the end of the year the child turns 15 years old.
2) At least $100 must have been contributed to the child's RESP account in at least four different years prior to the year she turns 16 years old.

The difference between these two conditions is that the first one can be met by contributing the $2,000 over any numbers of years. The second one involves making contributions of at least $100, in at least four different calendar years.

The last year you can open a first RESP for a child and expect to receive any grants is during the year when the child turns 15. You need to contribute $2,000 that year in order for the child to be eligible for grants in the years he turns 16 and 17.

**Just to clarify** – The ages mentioned previously refer to the calendar year in which the child turns the appropriate age. If you have to *make a contribution in the year the child turns 15*, this means the contribution has to be made at some point between January 1 and December 31 of that year. In fact, the child might be 14 at the time of contribution if it takes place before the child's birthday.

The last year you can start an RESP, make four annual $100 contributions and still be eligible for grants when the child is 16 and 17 is the year the child turns 12.

These age rules are important to know because if your child turns 15

35

this year and you are still thinking of opening an RESP for them, you need to act soon. It is still worthwhile to open an RESP in the year they turn 15. If you contribute $5,000 per year in the years they turn 15, 16 and 17, the grant total will be $3,000.

Let's look at an example of each rule:

**A total of $2,000 must be contributed towards the child's RESP by the end of the year in which the child turns 15 years old.**

Steven turns 15 years old in 2010. His parents decide to open an RESP account and contribute $5,000 per year for three years until Steven is not eligible for RESP grants anymore.

His parents contribute $5,000 in 2010, which is the year Steven turns 15. This means that the eligibility criteria for grants in the years he turns 16 and 17 is met. He will receive the full grants in the years where he turns 16 and 17.

**At least $100 must have been contributed to the child's RESP account in at least four different years prior to the year he turns 16 years old.**

Susie is turning 16 in 2010. Her parents have an RESP account for her but are not sure if she is still eligible to receive grants this year and in 2011.

Her parents check their statements and determine how much they have contributed in the past:

| | |
|------|---------------------|
| 2002 | $50 |
| 2004 | $500 |
| 2005 | $100 |
| 2006 | $200 |
| 2009 | $100 |
| 2010 | Year Susie turns 16 |

As you can see, there are four different years where at least $100 was contributed to the RESP account. This condition is met and Susie will be eligible for RESP grants in the years she turns 16 and 17 years of age.

36

# Chapter 3 Summary

The basic RESP grant is 20% of contributions, up to a maximum of $500 per year. A contribution of $2,500 will result in a $500 grant.

Additional grants are available for lower income families.

The maximum grant amount was only $400 (from a $2,000 contribution) in 2006 and prior years.

RESP contributions are not tax-deductible, so there will be no tax receipt issued and the contributions cannot be deducted from your taxable income.

Grants can be paid from when the child is born, up to the end of the year in which she turns 17.

The maximum lifetime grant amount payable to a beneficiary is $7,200.

Contributions that are in excess of the grant limits are allowed, but no grant will be paid.

The lifetime contribution limit per beneficiary is $50,000.

One year of prior contribution room can be used each calendar year, in addition to the current year's contribution room.

Contribution room is based on calendar years - not birthdates.

Contribution amounts and payment methods are very flexible.

In family plan accounts with two or more beneficiaries, the grant allocation between the beneficiaries must be specified.

There are special grant rules for years where the beneficiary is turning 16 or 17 years of age.

# 4

# RESP WITHDRAWAL RULES WHEN CHILD ATTENDS POST-SECONDARY EDUCATION

*Topics covered in this chapter:*

- *Requirements for eligible post-secondary schools*
- *RESP withdrawal procedure*
- *Withdrawing contributions and accumulated income*
- *Tax scenarios*

## Eligible post-secondary schooling

RESPs are intended to be used for valid post-secondary education. The eligibility rules are fairly lenient: It doesn't have to be a college or university education and it doesn't have to be full-time.

Here are the basic criteria for eligible full-time post-secondary schooling, as well as a phone number to verify if the school you are planning to attend is eligible.

- Enrolled for 10 hours per week or more
- Schooling is at least three consecutive weeks in length
- Enrolled at an eligible post-secondary institution
- Correspondence and trade programs are eligible
- Student cannot be employed full-time

To confirm that an educational institution qualifies, call the Canada Revenue Agency general enquiries telephone service at 1-800-959-8281. Select the option to speak to an agent.

*See Chapter 10: Part-Time Studies RESP Rules, for details about using an RESP to fund part-time studies.*

The educational facility does not have to be in Canada. While the beneficiaries must be Canadian residents in order to qualify for RESP grants, it is perfectly all right for the student to study abroad.

It is a good idea to verify the course eligibility in advance of enrolment, so there are no surprises.

**How to withdraw money from an RESP account**

Once the child is enrolled in an eligible post-secondary institution, the subscriber can start withdrawing money from the RESP account.

41

To withdraw money, you have to provide some proof to your RESP provider that the RESP beneficiary (child) is enrolled at an approved post-secondary school.

Contact your financial institution to find out the exact proof you need. Typically you might need to show proof of registration, a fees invoice or course schedule. You will need to show this proof every time you make a withdrawal from the RESP account.

The subscriber (owner) of the account is always in charge of the funds in the RESP account. They make the decisions about payments to the student. Money can be paid out to the student or the subscriber. You can request a cheque or set up an Electronic Funds Transfer (EFT) to your bank account or the student's bank account.

While the exact process for withdrawals may vary between financial institutions, the subscriber of the account has to contact the RESP provider, provide proof of enrolment and ask them to send money.

**Which expenses are eligible for RESP withdrawals?**

**All of them are.**

You should not have to justify any withdrawals from the RESP. You don't have to specify what the money will be spent on, and you don't have to show receipts. The money is for the child's education expenses, which means that any money spent while in school can be paid from the RESP. Tuition, textbooks, housing, transportation, computers, televisions or vacations are all eligible. Anything goes.

The government requirements state that it is up to the RESP provider to ensure that the money is used to further the student's education. It's possible that your financial institution might question you if you clean out the RESP account in the second term of school. If the institution complains, I suggest you argue and keep after them to get the money. If that doesn't happen, just try to take out as much as you are allowed. There is no harm in asking for as much as you can.

42

# *Specific Withdrawal Rules*

There are two main types of RESP withdrawal scenarios. The first type is when money is being withdrawn from the RESP account to be used by the beneficiary for their educational costs. The second type is when the subscriber decides to collapse the RESP plan, usually because the beneficiary has decided not to pursue post-secondary education.

Before we get into the specific withdrawal rules, we need to clarify some terms specific to RESP accounts.

**Contribution amount**

The **contribution** amount for any RESP account refers to the sum of all the contributions made to the account over the years. It doesn't matter if the investment value has gone up or down, the contribution amounts stay the same.

**Accumulated income amount**

The **accumulated income** amount is made up of the RESP government grants, capital gains,[3] interest payments, and dividend payments earned in the account. In other words, any money in the account that is not a contribution is considered to be accumulated income.

> **Example of contribution amount and accumulated income amount**
>
> Joe contributed $1,200 per year for 10 years to an RESP account he set up for his niece. 20% grants were paid on all the contributions and the investments have gone up in value. The account is now worth $17,000.
>
> His total contributions are $12,000 (10 times $1,200).

3   **Capital gains** is equal to any increase in value of your investments.

43

> The accumulated income amount is $5,000 ($17,000 minus $12,000).
>
> If the account has gone down in value and the accumulated income amount is zero or negative, the accumulated income amount is considered to be zero.

## Withdrawal Rules If Child Attends Post-Secondary Education

There are two types of withdrawals you can make from an RESP account when your child is going to school.

### 1 Post-Secondary Education Payments (PSE)

These payments are taken from the *contribution amount* portion of the RESP account. These payments are not taxable. There are no limits to the amount of contributions that can be withdrawn once the child is attending post-secondary education.

### 2 Educational Assistance Payments (EAP)

These payments are from the *accumulated income* portion of the RESP account. EAP payments are taxable in the hands of the student. There are no withholding taxes on EAP payments. If the student is expecting to pay income tax that year, he should set money aside to pay his tax bill the following year.

Only $5,000 of the accumulated income portion of your RESP account can be withdrawn in the first thirteen weeks of school. After the initial thirteen weeks, there is no limit to the amount of accumulated income that can be withdrawn.

Most students have enough tuition and education tax credits and a low enough income that they will likely pay very little or no income tax as a result of RESP withdrawals during their post-secondary education.

There are situations where managing these withdrawal types can lower the student's taxes. You should consult a tax professional for advice if necessary.

44

When withdrawing funds from your RESP, always direct your financial institution as to how much of the withdrawal should be from contributions (PSE) and how much should be from accumulated income (EAP).

**TIP:**
Note that in a family plan, grant money can be shared between beneficiaries, but the $7,200 lifetime limit must be respected. If you are completing withdrawals from a family plan, be careful not to pay more than $7,200 of grant money to any one beneficiary or the government will claim the excess grants back.

To avoid excess grant payment, ask your financial institutions for updates on how much grant money is paid to each beneficiary.

**Specific tax situations to be aware of:**

**Scenario One:** Co-operative education

The student is in a co-op program and has two work terms in one calendar year. This might result in an income high enough to pay taxes. Consider lowering the amount of accumulated income withdrawn that year (EAP) to minimize the tax impact.

**Scenario Two:** Summer job before school

Another situation is that when the student first starts school, she will have just completed a short summer (two months) and probably won't have much income for that year. One possible strategy is to take out extra EAP (accumulated income) to take advantage of the personal exemption, as well as tuition credits.

If the student makes a lot of money from his summer jobs, try to take out more accumulated income in years when the student's income is low and less accumulated income in years where the student's income is high. Accumulated income is taxable in the hands of the student in the year it is withdrawn.

If the student doesn't earn much money, take out more of the accumulated income in order to avoid any big tax bills when the child finishes school and the RESP has to be collapsed. The goal is to deplete the accumulated income portion of the RESP by the time the student finishes school.

**TIP:**
If you end up with too much money in the RESP and the child is still attending school, take out all the money when you can. If you leave it in the RESP account, you will eventually have to collapse it and pay extra taxes on it.

In an ideal world, you would just make the withdrawals as needed and take the last bit of money out just before she graduates. Any income earned on money in your RESP is not taxable, so it's best to leave it in the RESP as long as possible.

In the real world, however, it is possible that the student ends up not graduating or finishing school.

If you are worried about this possibility, you might want to think about withdrawing the money from the RESP as fast as possible and saving it in a high interest savings account. Yes, you will end up paying more in taxes because the interest payments are taxable income, but this will be less expensive than the penalties owed if you have to collapse the RESP. If this money is stored in a TFSA account, the interest payments will not be taxable.

Financial institutions will default your RESP withdrawals to *EAP*, which means they will pay out the accumulated income portion of the RESP before the contribution portion. This is in your best interest because it will help to avoid having too much accumulated income in the RESP when the child finishes school.

### Making Educational Assistance Payments (EAPs) if the child quits or finishes school

In 2008, the federal government made a rule change which allows EAPs (payments for education) to be made for up to six months after the student finishes or quits school. If necessary, make sure you take advantage of this rule. It is less costly to make an EAP to the student than it is to make an AIP (accumulated income payment) to the subscriber, which is what happens if you collapse the RESP. This is because if you collapse an RESP, the accumulated income becomes taxable income in the hands of the subscriber, plus there is a 20% penalty.

46

## Chapter 4 Summary

Post-secondary educational facility and program has to be eligible for RESP payments.

Eligibility requirements for schools and programs are very lenient. To confirm that an educational institution qualifies, call the General Enquiries telephone service at 1-800-959-8281.

The educational facility does not have to be located in Canada.

To get a payment from an RESP account, the subscriber must make a request to the financial institution and show proof of enrolment.

The subscriber controls the RESP account and decides when payments will be made and how much the payments will be for.

Any kind of expense is eligible for RESP payments. You don't have to show receipts.

Withdrawals will be either:

> PSE – Post-Secondary Education Payment. These are from the contribution portion of the RESP account and are not taxable.

> EAP – Educational Assistance Payment. These payments are from the *Accumulated Income* portion of the RESP account and are taxable in the hands of the student.

A maximum of $5,000 of PSE payments can be made from your RESP account during the first 13 weeks of school.

When doing RESP payments, specify to the financial institution if the payment is PSE, EAP or both.

# 5

# WITHDRAWAL RULES IF CHILD DOES NOT ATTEND POST-SECONDARY EDUCATION

*Topics covered in this chapter:*

- *How to collapse an RESP account*
- *Calculating collapse penalties*
- *Strategies for avoiding collapse penalty tax*

What happens if the student decides that school is not for him? There are a number of different options for dealing with the RESP account.

**Collapse the RESP account**

*Collapsing the RESP account* means you cash it in and take the net proceeds, which belong to you, the subscriber. This process involves taxes and penalties.

Here's how it works:

**Contribution amount:** Can be withdrawn with zero penalties or taxes.

**Grants:** RESP grants deposited in the account have to be paid back to the government. Your RESP provider will handle this by removing the grant money from your RESP account and sending the money to the government.

**Remainder of accumulated income:** This would include any money earned in the account such as capital gains, interest payments and dividends. The **accumulated income amount** is considered taxable income in the hands of the subscriber and will be added to your net taxable income in the year you collapse the account. In addition, a 20% tax will also be applied to this amount. This payment is called the AIP - *accumulated income payment.*

Penalties applied when collapsing an RESP account are harsh, but they are only applied to the accumulated income amount. No penalties or taxes are applied to the contribution amount.

This type of withdrawal can only be done if the beneficiaries are at least 21 and the account has been in existence for at least 10 years. Otherwise, you will only get the contribution amount back.

**RESP collapse example:**

Susan contributed $10,000 to her son's RESP over several years. $2,000 worth of RESP grants were paid into the account, and the total account value is now $17,000. Her marginal tax rate[4] is 43%.

Her son decides to join the circus, and Susan collapses the RESP.

The government gets $2,000, which is the amount of RESP grants paid into the account. Susan can withdraw the $10,000 of contributions with no penalties. There is $5,000 of accumulated income remaining, which has to be paid out. The accumulated income payout is taxable income for Susan, so she will pay 43% income tax plus 20% penalty tax for a total of 63%, which is $3,150. Her net payout from the accumulated income portion of the account is $1,850.

Out of the original $17,000 account value, Susan will get $11,850.

These penalties may seem severe, but it is important to note that the RESP grants that get taken back by the government never belonged to the subscriber. They are placed in the RESP account so that the subscriber can invest them along with the rest of the RESP funds. The subscriber is really just *holding* the grants for the future student. If the student doesn't use them, the grants go back to the government.

The 20% penalty is supposed to reflect the fact that some of the accumulated income is the result of the RESP grants, which are never owned by the subscriber. It is also intended to undo some of the tax-free accumulation that has occurred in the account.

There are other options to avoid the taxes if your child does not attend post-secondary education

**Transfer the AIP to you or your spouse's RRSP**

The taxes on the accumulated income payment are pretty severe. However, if you have RRSP room available, you are allowed to contribute the AIP, up to $50,000, to your RRSP or your spouse's RRSP. This means there will be no income tax immediately payable

---

4    Marginal tax rate is the tax rate applied to the last dollar earned in a year

on the AIP and the 20% extra tax will not be charged.

In Susan's case she has lots of unused RRSP room. She would be better off contributing the $5,000 AIP to her RRSP. Instead of receiving $1,850 in cash outside her RRSP, she will have $5,000 inside her RRSP.

If Susan needs the money from the RESP account and doesn't want to leave it in an RRSP for her retirement, she can still contribute the AIP to her RRSP. After a year, she can withdraw that money. It will be taxable income, but she will save the 20% extra penalty. This does use some RRSP contribution room, but if Susan wasn't planning to use all her RRSP room, it shouldn't matter.

There is a limit of $50,000 of AIP that can be contributed to the RRSP.

Here are the necessary conditions in order to transfer the AIP to an RRSP account:

- Subscriber is a resident of Canada
- Payment has to be made to only one subscriber of the plan
- Plan has been open for at least 10 years, and each individual who is or was a beneficiary, is over 21 years of age and not eligible for an educational assistance payment (EAP)

---

**Contribute AIP to RRSP example:**

Susan contributes the $5,000 AIP to her RRSP this year and then withdraws $5,000 from her RRSP the following year. Assuming she is still in the 43% marginal tax bracket, her net withdrawal after tax will be $2,850, which is a lot better than the $1,850 she would get by collapsing the RESP and paying the 20% extra tax.

---

**What if my spouse and I don't have any RRSP contribution room?**

No problem. If you are still working, then just wait until the following year to collapse your RESP. Reduce your RRSP contributions to create enough contribution room for the following year to contribute the accumulated income portion of the RESP. In

53

this case you are only saving the 20% penalty since you are reducing your normal RRSP contribution by an amount equal to the AIP. Saving 20% is still very worthwhile.

**More options if the child does not attend post-secondary school**

**Wait**. RESP accounts don't have to be terminated until 35 years after they are created. Unless you really need the money, waiting for a few years is a good idea. It's always possible that your child will give up on their pro hockey or music career and will use the money for schooling later on. If you don't meet the age and time criteria for withdrawing the AIP, waiting is a must.

Another benefit of waiting is that it allows more possibilities to reduce income taxes. As discussed previously, contributing the AIP to an RRSP will eliminate the 20% penalty. If you withdraw that money from your RRSP in a year when your income is significantly lower, the income taxes payable on the withdrawal might also be lower. This might be a situation where someone is retired and getting a portion of their income from an investment account. It could also apply to someone who has a lower income because they were unemployed for a time.

**Transfer to sibling**

You are allowed to transfer the RESP money to a sibling. This sibling could be part of the same family plan or in a different individual RESP account. The $7,200 lifetime grant limit still applies. If the transferred grants plus the grants the receiving sibling has already received exceed $7,200 then the excess grants have to be returned to the government.

If you have two children, and the older one seems to be on a non-educational path, you can think about cutting back contributions for him and possibly reducing contributions for the younger sibling in order to have enough room to transfer the grants from the older child to the younger sibling.

**The last option is donating the accumulated income**

In this case you can donate the AIP to a qualifying educational

54

institute. A payment to a Canadian designated educational institution would be a gift and not a donation. Therefore, a tax receipt will not be issued to the subscriber or to the beneficiary.

If you want to collapse an RESP account which has been open for less than 10 years or for which any of the beneficiaries are under 21, the CRA website says the CRA may waive the conditions requiring that the plan has existed for 10 years and that each beneficiary be at least 21 years of age and ineligible to receive an EAP. For more information, contact the Registered Plans Directorate at the Canada Revenue Agency (CRA) at 1-800-267-3100.

**My son just quit University after one year and there is still money in the RESP - do I have to pay a penalty to collapse the account?**

The penalties and taxes will have to be paid, if you collapse the RESP account. However, the 2008 budget allowed for EAP withdrawals up to six months after the child stops going to school. EAP withdrawals are made when you withdraw the accumulated income from the RESP. These will be taxed in the hands of the student and won't incur any penalties. Empty the account as soon as possible. This strategy can only be used if the student has already enrolled in post-secondary education. It can't be used if the child never starts post-secondary education.

55

# Chapter 5 Summary

If the account is collapsed, the subscriber will be taxed on the non-contribution amount (AIP) at their marginal tax rate plus 20%.

Contributions will be returned to the subscriber with no taxes or penalties.

The accumulated income will only be returned if the beneficiaries are at least 21 and the account has been in existence for at least 10 years.

The extra 20% penalty can be avoided by transferring the accumulated income to your RRSP or your spouse's RRSP.

The accumulated income can be transferred to a sibling.

The RESP account does not have to be collapsed immediately.

# 6

# ADDITIONAL GRANTS FOR LOWER INCOME FAMILIES

*Topics covered in this chapter:*

- *Additional grant amounts*
- *Eligibility for additional grants*
- *Primary caregiver income determines eligibility*
- *Not all companies offer these grants*
- *How to apply for additional grants*
- *Canada Learning Bond*

The regular RESP grants (CESGs), calculated at 20% of contributions, are available to all eligible Canadians regardless of their individual or family income. It doesn't matter whether you earn $20 a year or $2,000,000 a year - you still qualify for the basic RESP grants.

Besides the 20% basic grant, the government offers additional grants based on family income.

There are a large number of middle (and lower) class Canadians who are eligible for these additional grants – and probably don't know about it.

The income levels for additional grants apply to the primary caregiver of the child and not the person who opens the account.

These additional RESP grants apply to the first $500 of contributions each year, unlike the normal RESP grants, which are payable on the first $2,500 of contributions per year.

There are two different income levels for these additional grants.[5] Families with a net income between $40,970 and $81,941 are eligible for an extra 10% grant on the first $500 of contributions each year for a total of $50 per year.

Families with a net income of $40,970 or less are eligible for an extra 20% grant on the first $500 of contributions each year for a total of $100 per year.

The *family income* in this case refers to the caregiver, who might not necessarily be the subscriber or owner of the account.

**Net income:** This is the amount on Line 236 of your T1 general tax form. It is your income net of RRSP contributions, child care expenses etc.

---

5    The updated income levels can be found at http://www. canlearn.ca/eng/saving/cesg/index.shtml, which is updated annually. The income values used in this book are for 2010.

Note that the $7,200 lifetime grant limit per beneficiary includes additional grants.

**Additional RESP Grants Example 1 - Higher income family**

Chris and Mary have a total family income of $90,000. After deducting $7,500 of RRSP contributions and $5,000 of child care expenses, they are left with a net income of $77,500. This is within the income range for the additional 10% RESP grant, which means they qualify for that additional grant.

By contributing $1,000 to an RESP account, they receive the basic grant of 20%, which is $200. Plus they receive an additional 10% on the first $500 of the contribution, which is $50. Their total grant on the $1,000 is $250.

| | |
|---|---|
| Net income of primary caregiver family = | $77,500 |
| RESP Contribution = | $1000 |
| Basic grant (20%) = | $200 |
| Additional 10% grant on first $500 = | $50 |
| **Total grant is** | **$250** |

**Additional RESP Grants Example 2 - Lower income family**

Susan and John have a net family income of $35,000. John's parents opened an RESP account for their granddaughter and contributed $1,000. The basic grant of 20% is $200. The family income of the primary caregiver is within the income range for the additional 20% grant, so they get another 20% grant on the first $500 of the contribution, which is $100 for a grand total of $300.

| | |
|---|---|
| Net income of primary caregiver family = | $35,000 |
| RESP Contribution = | $1000 |
| Basic grant (20%) = | $200 |
| Additional 20% grant on first $500 = | $100 |
| **Total grant is** | **$300** |

Lower income families are not as likely to make RESP contributions. However, the income qualification for additional grants is based on net family income of the primary caregiver. Someone with a higher income can open an RESP account for each child in a lower income family and receive the additional grants.

In this example, a grandparent opens an RESP for her grandchild and contributes $500 every year in order to receive the maximum additional grants. The primary caregiver's net income is $35,000.

The annual $500 contributions will earn the regular RESP grant of 20%, which is $100. They also receive another 20% additional grant, which is another $100. In total, there will be $200 of RESP grants paid every year. After 18 years, the contributions total $9,000 and the grants total $3,600, which is a lot of government money. This is a great deal!

**There are two steps you must take to get these additional grants:**

1) Make sure your financial institution offers these extra grants. RESPs are expensive to administer, and because of the limited size of the accounts, they are not a big source of profit for financial institutions. Administering the low income additional grants is even more work, and most companies don't offer these in self-directed accounts. You can ask your advisor or the financial institution where you are planning to open your RESP if they offer addition RESP grants. You can also check out the CRA list of promoters who offer extra grants.[6]

2) Fill out the parts of the SDE 0071 RESP application forms which apply to the additional grants. This form is used for someone who is applying only for regular RESP grants as well as additional grants.

Make sure you inform your financial institution that you are applying for the additional grants, and they will help you with the proper forms.

---

6   http://www.hrsdc.gc.ca/eng/learning/education_savings/ publicsection/new_promoter_list.shtml

61

You can apply for additional RESP grants retroactively for up to three years after you make the contribution.

If you are opening an RESP account and you are not the primary caregiver for the child, you need the primary caregiver to fill out the appropriate sections of the form in order to get the regular CESG as well as apply for the additional CESG. See Chapter 11: How to Get Your RESP Account Started for more information about setting up an RESP account.

## Canada Learning Bond

The Canada Learning Bond (CLB) is a special kind of RESP grant available to lower income Canadians. The CLB grant is special because no RESP contributions have to be made to receive it. Eligible applicants just have to open an RESP account, and apply for the CLB grant.

### Eligibility for the Canada Learning Bond (CLB)

- Primary caregiver has to receive the National Child Benefit Supplement (NCBS). This supplement is generally for families with a net annual income below $37,178. You don't have to receive it continuously, but will only get the CLB for years where you receive the NCBS.
- Child has to be born in 2004 or after.

The following link contains more information about the National Child Benefit Supplement http://www.nationalchildbenefit.ca/.

### How much is the Canada Learning Bond grant?

The Canada Learning Bond pays an initial $500 in the first year and then pays $100 per year up to 15 years for a possible total of $2,000. The first payment includes an extra $25 to cover account opening costs, so the first year's payment is $525.

### How do I get this CLB grant?

The process to get this grant is the same as for the additional RESP

62

grants. Just set up an RESP account at a financial institution that offers the CLB. Here is the link showing the financial companies which offer the CLB:

- http://www.hrsdc.gc.ca/eng/learning/education_savings/ publications_resources/promoter/forms/sde0071/index. shtml

When you fill out the RESP application form (SDE 0071), make sure you apply for the Canada Learning Bond.

These are links to more information about the CLB:

- http://www.hrsdc.gc.ca/eng/learning/education_savings/ public/clb.shtml
- http://www.canlearn.ca/eng/saving/clb/brochure/clb. shtml

**TIP:**

This grant can also be paid into an RESP account for a subscriber who does not meet the eligibility requirements because they make too much money. The eligibility is determined by the primary caregiver of the child.

For example: Let's say Uncle John makes $400,000 per year. His nephew's mom works as a starving artist and has a very low income. Dad is not in the picture. If Uncle John sets up an RESP and lists his sister as the primary caregiver for the nephew, the account will be eligible for the additional RESP grants based on the low family income of the child. Uncle John's income is not relevant.

## Chapter 6 Summary

Families with net income of lower than $81,941 can qualify for up to $50 of additional grants per year.

Families with net income of lower than $40,970 can qualify for up to $100 of additional grants per year.

Only $500 of contributions per year is necessary to get the maximum RESP additional grants.

The additional grants are based on the primary caregiver's net family income.

Not all financial institutions offer these extra grants. If you are eligible for additional grants, make sure you ask before setting up an account.

# 7

# ALBERTA CENTENNIAL EDUCATION SAVINGS (ACES) GRANTS

*Topics covered in this chapter:*

- *Amounts and timing of grants*
- *Eligibility for ACES grants*

Alberta Centennial Education Savings (ACES) grants are grants that can be paid to current and former residents of Alberta.

Here is the basic outline of this program:

- No contribution required
- $500 initial one-time grant
- Three subsequent payments of $100 payable at ages 8, 11 and 14
- No income test for ACES grants

The initial grant and subsequent grants have different eligibility requirements:

### Eligibility for the initial $500 ACES grant

- Child must be born in 2005 or later
- Child has a parent or guardian who is a resident of Alberta at the time of application, or at the time of birth
- Child has an RESP account set up where she is named as a beneficiary
- Application must be made within six years of the child's birth

### Eligibility for the subsequent $100 ACES grants

- Child has an RESP account setup in which he is named as a beneficiary
- Child turns 8, 11 or 14 in 2005 or later
- Child has a parent or guardian who is a resident of Alberta at the time of application, or at the time of the child's applicable birthday
- Child is attending school at the time of application, or at the time of the child's applicable birthday
- A contribution of at least $100 must be made to an RESP

67

with the child named as a beneficiary within one year prior to application
- Application must be made within six years after the relevant birthdays

The key difference between the initial $500 ACES grant and the subsequent $100 ACES grants is that the $500 grant does not require a contribution into the RESP account. The $100 grants are all dependent on having a $100 contribution made by the subscriber into the RESP account first.

The following link contains more information on the ACES program: http://aet.alberta.ca/planning/funding/aces.aspx

The grants can be paid into an RESP with a subscriber who is not eligible for RESP grants. It is the primary caregiver of the child who determines eligibility for the RESP grants.

The process to get this grant is the same as the process for the additional RESP grants. You have to open an RESP account at a financial institution that offers the ACES grant and fill out the proper form. Here is the link showing which companies offer ACES:

http://www.hrsdc.gc.ca/eng/learning/education_savings/publicsection/new_promoter_list.shtml

# Chapter 7 Summary

ACES grants are a $500 initial payment and up to three subsequent payments of $100 payable at ages 8, 11 and 14.

Alberta residency is determined by the parent at the time of application or at the time of the child's applicable birthday.

The $100 grants require a $100 initial RESP contribution.

# 8
# QUEBEC RESP GRANTS (QESI)

*Topics covered in this chapter:*

- *QESI grant rules*
- *Supplemental grants for lower income families*
- *How to qualify*

The government of Quebec has created a provincial educational savings grant program called QESI (Quebec Education Savings Incentive). These grants are paid to Quebec residents on top of the normal federal RESP grants. QESI grants will be paid into the same account as the federal RESP grants, so you don't need to open a separate account.

### Quebec QESI grant rules

The maximum QESI grant amount per year is calculated at 10% of the first $2,500 contributed per beneficiary. The highest amount of QESI grants a beneficiary can receive in one year is $250.

The lifetime maximum grant amount per beneficiary is $3,600.

There is a $250 grant carry forward (as of 2008), so you can actually contribute $5,000 to your RESP and get a $500 QESI grant if you have enough contribution room. This applies to all years from 2008 and onward.

### Supplemental increase for lower income families

Families with a net income of $38,385 or less can receive extra grants of 10% of net contributions up to a maximum of $50 per beneficiary per tax year.

Families with a net income between $38,385 and $76,770 qualify for extra grants of 5% of net contributions up to a maximum of $25 per beneficiary per tax year.

The supplemental QESI grant is payable only to an RESP that is either an individual plan or a family plan where all the beneficiaries are siblings.

### Contribution space, or accumulated rights

Every eligible child begins to receive QESI contribution room at birth or on February 21, 2007, whichever is later. The Quebec government has termed grant room for the QESI basic amount as *accumulated rights*.

The QESI grant rights accumulate at a rate of $250 per year. As of 2008, any QESI rights accumulated during previous years can be added to the basic amount up to a maximum of $500 a year.

The supplementary QESI credit cannot be carried forward if not used. The carry forward only applies to the basic QESI grant.

### Example of QESI grants for medium income family

Pierre and Gabrielle just had a baby and want to open an RESP account. They want to know how much in RESP and QESI grants they are eligible for each year.

| | |
|---|---|
| Net family income = | $60,000 |
| Annual contribution amount = | $2,500 |
| Basic federal RESP grant of 20% = | $500 |
| Additional federal RESP grant of 10% on first $500 contribution because of income = . | $50 |
| Basic QESI grant of 10% = | $250 |
| Supplemental QESI grant of 5% on first $500 contribution because of income = | $25 |

Bottom line:

The maximum grants they can get each year, assuming their net income doesn't change drastically, is $825 on a contribution of $2,500 each year.

### Eligibility requirements for Quebec QESI grants

The eligibility requirements for QESI grants are the same as the eligibility requirements for the federal government RESP grant. See Chapter 2: *RESP Account Rules* for eligibility requirements.

**QESI beneficiary eligibility criteria**

Every child up to and including age 17 is eligible to receive the QESI grant, provided the child meets all of these requirements:

- Child is Quebec resident as of December 31st in the taxation year being applied for
- Child has a valid Social Insurance Number (SIN)
- Child is named as a beneficiary to an RESP where the QESI is offered
- Child meets the CESG 16/17 year-old rules
- Child has a contribution made to an RESP in their name
- Child has available grant room

You don't need to apply for the QESI because your financial institution should do it for you. Always verify that you are getting the proper amounts once you start receiving grant payments.

## Chapter 8 Summary

Quebec has special RESP grants called QESI grants, paid on top of the normal federal grants.

QESI grants are paid into a regular RESP account.

The maximum QESI grant payable is $250 per year. This is calculated at 10% of the first $2,500 of contributions.

Lower income families are eligible for an extra $50 of QESI grants per year, per beneficiary.

A child's contribution room starts accumulating on February 21, 2007 or at birth, whichever is later.

# 9
# CANADIAN RESIDENCY RESP ELIGIBILITY RULES

*Topics covered in this chapter:*

- *Residency of the subscriber*
- *Residency of the beneficiary*

The Canadian residency rules[7] for RESPs can be confusing because there are at least two parties involved with an RESP account -- the subscriber and one or more beneficiaries.

The residency of the beneficiary is important because it determines if an RESP account can be opened and if it is eligible for contributions and RESP grants. The residency of the subscriber does not impact grants eligibility.

### Residency of the subscriber

The person opening the account does not have to be a Canadian resident, but they have to have a valid Social Insurance Number (SIN). A non-resident subscriber can open an RESP account, make contributions, receive grants and initiate withdrawals.

The tax-sheltered status of the RESP only applies to Canadian residents. If the subscriber or account owner is a non-resident, they might have to pay taxes on any income earned in the RESP account as well as capital gains, according to the rules of their resident country.

### Residency of the beneficiary or child

The beneficiary of an RESP account must be a Canadian resident with a valid SIN in order to:

- Open an RESP account
- Make contributions to the account
- Receive RESP grants in the account
- Withdraw money from the RESP while going to school

If the beneficiary of an RESP account becomes a non-resident, the

---

7   Here is a link to the CRA residency definition: http://www.cra-arc.gc.ca/tx/nnrsdnts/cmmn/rsdncy-eng.html.

account can be kept intact, but no contributions can be made and grants are not paid. If the beneficiary moves back to Canada and re-establishes Canadian residency, contributions can again be made and grants will be paid on contributions. No grant room will be accumulated for the time during which the beneficiary was a non-resident.

If the beneficiary has moved away from Canada and it is likely the beneficiary will be returning to Canada, it makes sense to keep the RESP account in place. If the beneficiary is not coming back to Canada, collapsing the account should be considered.

To use the RESP money for post-secondary education, the beneficiary must be a Canadian resident. The student can attend either a Canadian post-secondary school or a non-Canadian school as long as they maintain their Canadian residency during their school years.

# Chapter 9 Summary

The subscriber does not have to be a Canadian resident in order for RESP grants to be paid to the RESP account.

The subscriber must have a valid SIN to open an RESP account.

The beneficiary must be a Canadian resident in order for RESP grants to be paid into the RESP account.

If the beneficiary is not a Canadian resident, an existing RESP account can be maintained - but no contributions can be made.

The beneficiary must be a Canadian resident in order to receive payments from the RESP accounts.

The tax-sheltered status of the RESP does not apply if the subscriber is a non-resident. Local tax rules will apply.

# 10
# PART-TIME STUDIES RESP RULES

*Topics covered in this chapter:*

- *Rule differences for part-time studies RESP*
- *Eligibility for part-time studies*

Funds in an RESP account can also be used for part-time post-secondary studies. The rules are different for part-time students.

- The student must be at least 16 years old
- The educational program must last at least three consecutive weeks and require at least 12 hours of instruction each month for the duration of the program
- The educational program must be at a post-secondary level
- The government term for a qualifying program is *specified education program*

The Educational Assistance Payment (EAP) system is also slightly different. Remember that EAP is the accumulated income portion of your RESP account.

In any 13 week period of enrolment, the maximum amount of EAP payments that can be paid to a beneficiary is $2,500.

Unlike full-time students, part-time students have an EAP limit for the duration of the program instead of just the first 13 weeks.

**RESP part-time studies example**

Susie is enrolled part-time and withdraws a $2,000 EAP on June 1, 2010.

On August 1, she decides to take out more EAP. Because the $2,000 withdrawal was completed less than 13 weeks ago, she can only withdraw $500 of EAP since the maximum is $2,500 for any 13 week period.

On September 1, she wants more money and calculates that she can withdraw $2,000 because the $500 August 1 payment is within 13 weeks of September 1. The original $2,000 withdrawal on June 1 was completed more than 13 weeks ago and therefore is not included in the limit.

# Chapter 10 Summary

Payments from an RESP account can be used for eligible part-time studies.

The maximum EAP (non-contributions) payment to the beneficiary is only $2,500 in any 13 week period of enrolment.

# 11
# HOW TO GET YOUR RESP ACCOUNT STARTED

*Topics covered in this chapter:*

- *Requirements for opening an RESP account*
- *Different options for opening an account*
- *Using a big bank*
- *Do it yourself investing*

The next step is to get started by opening up an RESP account and contributing some money.

Before trying to open an RESP account, make sure you have:

1) A SIN for the child
2) A SIN for the person opening up the account

**How and where do I open an RESP account?**

There are several different options for setting up an RESP account. I'm going to list some of the more common methods, and then we'll take a closer look at a couple of the better ones for details on how to actually get an RESP account setup.

**A big bank**

Most bank branches have the personnel on hand to help you open an RESP account and select investments.

- **Pros** - Super easy, especially if you already bank there. Banks will help you with the documentation and get you set up.
- **Cons** - The RESP and investing expertise of the person you are dealing with might not be very high. Another issue is that you will be buying bank investment products, which likely mean that the fees will be fairly high. There are exceptions: TD, RBC and National Bank all have low-cost index funds available with annual management costs of less than 1%.

**Do-It-Yourself Investing**

This is my favourite method, but it is not for everyone. For do-it-yourself investors, I suggest looking at the TD e-funds series, which are the cheapest mutual funds in Canada.

- **Pros** - Cheap, cheap, cheap! Annual costs of TD e-funds are much less than most mutual funds.

89

- **Cons** – More work. More hassle. You have to know something about investing, and you need to be interested in managing your own RESP account.

### Using a financial advisor or financial planner

These individuals are trained to help you with your investments. They can assist you with opening up accounts and provide guidance as to which investments to buy. Most advisors work on commission, so you don't pay them directly. The money for their commissions comes from the mutual funds they will want you to invest in.

- **Pros** - Easy. The financial advisor or planner does all the research and gets the paperwork ready for you to sign.
- **Cons** - High fees. While they don't charge directly, the advisor will usually make an on-going commission from any investments you buy through them. Lack of knowledge of specific RESP rules might also be a problem with some advisors.

The biggest problem is that they often won't accept clients with less than a certain dollar figure of investible assets. You might have to use the advisor for other investment accounts such as RRSPs in order for them to take you on as a client.

Fee-only advisors can be cheaper, but only if you have enough assets. Most RESP accounts are not large enough to benefit from any savings by using a fee-only advisor.

Another type of financial advisor is really just a mutual fund salesperson. These people have very little training and although you might feel safer investing with one, you might as well just do it yourself. Ask the salesperson what his or her title and qualifications are. If the IFIC (Investment Funds Institute of Canada) is the only qualification mentioned, they are a mutual fund salesperson.

### Scholarship/Pooled/Group RESP plans

These plans are very structured and typically are *sold* by salespeople. Most hospital maternity wards have pamphlets advertising these companies.

- **Pros** - Easy.

90

- **Cons** – Very, very expensive. There are large upfront sales fees paid to the salesperson, which are paid from your contributions, and very high ongoing fees. They have restrictive rules that can mean getting less money out of the plan if the child doesn't go to school.

If you have one of these RESP plans, you should contact the RESP provider to find out which rules they have placed on top of the regular federal RESP rules.

My suggestion for the average Canadian who doesn't already have an investment advisor is to use one of the major banks or just do it yourself.

Using your current bank to open an RESP is probably the most convenient choice for most people, which is a positive since it means the account is more likely to get set up. The fees at banks and other investment companies do add up, but for small investment accounts like RESPs that have a finite life span, paying higher fees is not the end of the world. Some banks do offer lower cost mutual or index funds, but you have to research and ask for them. TD, RBC and National Bank all have low-cost index funds available with annual management costs of less than 1%.

**Bottom line:** It is a lot better to use your bank or financial advisor to get the account started now rather than procrastinate and never get one started.

### Two Critical bits of investing information to know

**Asset allocation** - Make sure your asset allocation is appropriate for your timeline. If you are using a financial advisor, make sure he explains the asset allocation in the account to you.

**Fees** - All mutual funds have published fees. It is up to you find out what they are or ask your advisor. Even if you use an advisor, you can still ask for cheaper funds.

### Setting up an RESP account at a major bank

It is very easy to open an RESP account at a bank. I would suggest calling the branch you deal with and setting up an appointment with

91

an investment professional. Tell them you wish to open an RESP account. When you have the meeting, there will be some discussion about what your risk tolerance is and some paperwork to fill out and sign. You should be able to get the account opened very quickly.

**TIP:** Watch out for annual account fees. Get them waived, if possible.

The reason I recommend using a bank over an investment advisor/planner is because the costs are roughly the same, and a busy financial planner is not likely to take on a new client who only wants to open an RESP account. Most investment professionals make their money based on a percentage of the assets under their control. RESP accounts are relatively small and complicated, so they are not as profitable for the financial planner.

Just because you have an investment professional working with you doesn't mean you can just set the account up and forget about it. You will still have to keep an eye on the account - the contributions as well as the asset allocation.

### Do-It-Yourself RESP investing

DIY investing means that you don't receive any kind of financial advice from anyone. You are responsible for setting up the RESP account, getting money into the account and selecting the investments. One thing to note is that most self-directed RESP accounts will not pay out any additional RESP grants for lower income families (the Canada Learning Bond, Alberta Aces grant or the Quebec QESI grant).

Here is a list of the various companies and the types of RESP grants they support:  http://www.hrsdc.gc.ca/eng/learning/education_savings/publicsection/new_promoter_list.shtml

In my opinion, the best deal for Canadian RESP do-it-yourself-ers is at TD bank. They have a series of index funds called *TD e-funds*, which have extremely low fees. In many cases the e-funds management fees are a quarter of most regular mutual funds.

The drawback of the TD e-funds account is that it is a bit of a hassle to set up, and only offers the basic RESP grant.

92

**Specific instructions for setting up a TD account for TD e-funds index funds**

1) Open a TD Mutual Funds RESP account at your nearest TD Canada Trust branch or by mail.
2) Make your initial contribution to the TD Mutual Fund account and purchase the TD Money Market fund. This is not an investment recommendation – it is just a place to park your money until you get the e-fund account established.
3) Convert the mutual fund account into a TD e-Series Funds account by applying to get your account converted into a TD e-Series Funds Account.
4) Switch out of the money market fund (which you purchased with your initial contribution) and put the money into a selection of low-cost e-funds.

**DIY option that is eligible for additional grants**

If the primary caregiver will be eligible for additional grants and you still want to DIY, one option to consider is to set up a TD Canada Trust Educational Savings Account in addition to the TD e-funds account. This account is eligible for additional grants and the CLB.

There are no annual fees and you can invest in GICs and mutual funds.

If you are eligible for additional grants, consider contributing $500 per year to the TD RESP account in order to get the maximum additional grants.

The second account will be the TD e-fund account where you will make the remainder of your contributions. This way you can get the additional RESP grants, and you can still own the ultra-cheap TD e-funds, keeping your investment costs to a minimum.

The downside of two RESP accounts is that they will be more work to open and manage.

93

# Chapter 11 Summary

To open an RESP account, you must have a valid SIN for yourself, as well as for the beneficiary.

There are many different places to open an RESP account: banks, financial advisors, online discount brokerages.

You can make your own investment decisions or hire an advisor.

The easiest place to set up an RESP is a big bank.

# 12

# BASIC INVESTING INFORMATION FOR RESP ACCOUNTS

*Topics covered in this chapter:*

- *Suggested reading*
- *Investment products for RESP accounts*
- *Investor risk profile*
- *Asset allocation*
- *Investment time horizon*

There are many options for investing in RESP accounts. You can buy guaranteed products like Guaranteed Investment Certificates (GICs), or you can keep your money in a high interest savings account, individual stocks, mutual funds, Exchange Traded Funds (ETFs) or index funds.

If you decide to use some sort of investment professional to help you open and manage your RESP, he or she will probably suggest investment products and asset allocation models for you. It is still important for you to know what investments you own in your RESP account and to be aware of the asset allocation as well.

If you plan to manage the RESP account yourself, this section will be a good introduction to investing, but I would suggest you do more reading on the topic.

My two recommendations are:

> *Four Pillars of Investing* by William Bernstein
>
> *Investor's Manifesto* by William Bernstein

*Four Pillars* is my favourite investment book of all time however it is a bit complicated and mathematical in a few sections. The *Investor's Manifesto* is a simplified version of *Four Pillars*, which might be useful for more Canadians. Both of these books focus on low-cost passive investing, which basically means buying low-cost index funds or exchange traded funds and not trying to time the market.

This chapter covers the very basics of investing and how to apply them to starting and managing an RESP account.

First, we'll cover possible investment products for your RESP. Then, we will discuss the topics of investing time horizon and asset allocation, which are necessary to be able to manage the RESP account effectively over time.

**Guaranteed Investment Certificates (GICs)**

GICs are a guaranteed investment in which you pay a set amount for the GIC and the bank will guarantee that you get your original money (principal) back when the GIC matures, plus a fixed interest rate. Because you are agreeing to leave the money with the bank for a certain amount of time, GICs tend to pay a higher interest rate than a normal savings account. The length of time from when you buy the GIC to maturity is called the *term*.

GICs are very safe – they are guaranteed by the financial institution and, more importantly, the Canadian Deposit Insurance Corporation (CDIC)[8] will guarantee any GICs you own up to $100,000 per bank. Credit Unions are covered under similar provincial guarantees.

GICs are considered to be fixed income investments. Even if you own mostly mutual funds, it helps to have some of your money allocated to a safer investment to weather any bear markets. GICs are also useful if you are saving for a particular large purchase such as a car (or a university tuition payment ;-), where you know you will need the money at a certain point in time.

One thing to be very aware of is the early withdrawal penalty. This penalty is usually several months of interest. If you buy a GIC, make sure you buy a term appropriate for you. If you are not sure of when you will need the money, buying a shorter term GIC is a good idea.

**High interest savings accounts**

High interest savings accounts offer a higher interest rate than a chequing account. In today's low inflation environment, the interest rates offered for these accounts may seem pretty low. It is important to understand that the inflation rate has to be taken into consideration as well.

If you invest money at 2% and inflation is 2%, in real terms, you

---

8    For more information on the CDIC, check out this website: http://www.cdic.ca/e/index.html

aren't gaining or losing purchasing power. For this reason, it doesn't matter how high or low the interest rates are as long as they are not being outpaced by inflation.

Risk level should be one of the biggest determining factors when deciding where to put your money. If you are saving for the long term, you can afford some risk. If you are saving for the short term, you can't afford any big losses, so the safety of the principal is more important than the interest earned on the investment. As your child gets older, the investing horizon gets shorter, so the *long term* eventually becomes the *short term*.

**Individual stocks**

Have you ever heard someone talking about a "hot stock tip" or "playing the markets"? Were you too embarrassed to admit that you don't really know what a stock is or how to buy one? Then keep reading!

Stocks are shares in companies. If you buy a share of a company – let's use Google as an example – you are now a part-owner of Google.

Does this mean you can enjoy a free lunch at the Google employee cafeteria? Of course not – large companies issue many shares, so if you only own a few, your *ownership* stake is very small. You normally get a vote for each share you own, so you do get some say in the management of the company.

Stocks are risky. This doesn't mean, however, that if you invest in stocks you will necessarily lose money. What it means is that because the stock price can go up or down, there is a chance that you might make money, break even or lose money on your investment. If you were to buy the stock of a company that eventually goes bankrupt, you could lose your entire investment.

You can buy stocks of individual companies in your RESP if you have an account at a discount stock brokerage. Many investors don't buy individual stocks, but would rather buy a mutual fund or index fund or exchange traded fund, which is like a basket of stocks. Some funds are managed by professional fund managers, whereas index funds and exchange traded funds are mostly based on stock market indexes.

**What is a stock market index?**

A stock market index (or just *index*) is a number that refers to the relative value of a group of stocks. As the stocks in this group change value, the index also changes value.

For example: An index might have a value of 1000 points at the beginning of the day. If the stocks in that index rise in value by 1% during the day, the index will be at 1010 points at the end of the day.

An example of a stock market index is the TSX 60 Index, which is based on the largest companies on the Toronto Stock Exchange.

**Index funds**

An index fund is a mutual fund that invests in the same stocks that are contained in a stock index, in the same proportion as that stock index.

Imagine a stock index — let's call it the RESP Index — that contains two stocks: Bank of Montreal and Telus. Let's say that the RESP Index is currently made up of 60% Bank of Montreal and 40% Telus. If an index fund is based on the RESP Index, it too will also invest in Bank of Montreal and Telus — 60% of the index fund will be invested in Bank of Montreal and 40% will be in Telus.

These percentages will change as the values of Bank of Montreal and Telus change. If the price of Bank of Montreal stock increases and the price of Telus stock decreases, the index will change so that maybe 65% will be Bank of Montreal and only 35% will be Telus.

One of the benefits of index funds is that the costs are lower than for managed mutual funds since there is no need to have expensive portfolio managers on the payroll.

**Watch out for index fund costs**

The original idea behind index funds was to provide a low-cost, passive alternative to traditional expensive mutual funds. However, there is no law that any index fund has to have low expenses, so make sure that you check the fund costs before investing. GlobeInvestor. com is my favourite site to research investment funds.

100

## Which stock market index?

Before investing in any index funds, make sure you know which index the fund is based on. Not all indexes are the same; some are very specific and might not be appropriate for your needs.

## Mutual funds

Mutual funds are investment funds that are run by a professional portfolio manager. The portfolio manager uses their knowledge and experience to decide what the best investments are for their mutual fund.

There are many different types of mutual funds, which can invest in different combinations of investments, depending on the type of the fund. All mutual funds will hold at least a small amount of cash in addition to their regular investments.

Here are some general types of mutual funds and the types of investments you might find in them:

- **Equity funds:** These usually hold stocks of various companies along with exchange traded funds and options in some cases.
- **Bond Funds:** These hold fixed income investments such as bonds and preferred shares.
- **Balanced funds:** A combination of equity and bond funds. These funds can hold any type of investment that an equity fund and bond fund can hold.
- **Target Retirement Funds:** Similar to balanced funds, but are geared toward a particular retirement date.

**Index funds** are also mutual funds. They are just a particular type of mutual fund.

There are also more specific types of funds available concentrating on a particular industry or geographic region. For example: A country-specific fund will only invest in companies from a particular country.

An industry-specific fund would be a fund that only invests in one industry such as oil. An oil based mutual fund might invest in oil producers, refineries, gas stations, etc.

101

The downside of managed mutual funds is the fees. They are normally taken directly out of the fund by the company that manages the fund. You will never see the fees charged directly.

Currency hedging is another possible feature of mutual funds. It is possible for example to buy a mutual fund that only invests in US stocks but is hedged so that fluctuations in the Canadian dollar/US dollar exchange rate don't affect the fund returns. This hedging feature comes with a cost and isn't always accurate.

### Bonds

Bonds, also known as **fixed income**, are an investment you can purchase in which you essentially lend money to whoever issued the bond in exchange for future income in the form of interest payments. At the end of the life of the bond, you get your original investment back. The interest payments and principal (amount of your investment) are guaranteed by the company or government that issued the bonds.

It is possible to buy bonds in your RESP account, but it is far more common to purchase mutual funds or index funds that contain bonds. A bond index fund or a balanced mutual fund which contains both stocks and bonds are two examples.

Bonds are considered a less risky investment compared to stocks because the interest payments and principal are guaranteed by the issuer. Typically, *safer* bonds that are issued by the Canadian government pay a lower interest rate, whereas *riskier* bonds issued by companies will pay a higher interest rate to compensate for the extra risk.

For bond mutual funds, it is very important to look at the costs since the extra benefit of having a portfolio manager is not as significant for bond mutual funds as it is for stock mutual funds.

Not all bonds or bond funds have the same amount of risk. When looking at a bond mutual fund, try to find out the *average duration* of the fund. The higher this number is, the more volatile the fund value can be if interest rates go up or down. If you desire less risk, look for a shorter duration such as three years or less.

102

### Exchange Traded Funds (ETF)

An ETF is an investment that contains the same stocks as a stock market index in the same proportion as that stock index. ETFs are very similar to index funds with respect to their investment methodology.

There are however, some very significant differences from the investor's point of view.

The biggest one is how they are purchased and sold. Index funds can be purchased without any trading fees, whereas exchange traded funds are bought and sold like individual company stocks, so there are trading fees every time you wish to buy or sell any ETFs.

Another way that ETFs are different from index funds is the ongoing costs. ETFs can have a less expensive management fee than index funds, which means that the ongoing costs of an ETF should be a bit lower than an equivalent index fund.

If you consider both management fees and the trading costs, the best choice really depends on the specific funds you are looking at, how much you are going to invest as well as your trading costs. Usually you need a fairly large portfolio to be able to take advantage of the (usually) lower costs of ETFs. As a simple rule of thumb – if you have less than $100,000 in total assets in the account, you are probably better off with index funds.

The vast majority of RESP accounts will be in the valuation range where index funds make more sense than exchange traded funds (ETFs).

**Automation of purchases:** One of the great advantages to index funds (and mutual funds in general) is that you can automate your purchases. If you want to contribute a certain dollar amount each month to a few different funds, automating that process allows you to *set it and forget it*. Once you set up the automated monthly purchases, money will be withdrawn from your bank account and the purchases will be made without you having to do anything. This is the single biggest reason why I think that most RESP investors should invest in index funds or mutual funds rather than ETFs, if they are planning to make regular purchases.

103

**Investor Risk Profile**

For some people, setting up their RESP account might be their first foray into the world of investing. Figuring out your risk profile is one of the key steps to managing an RESP account.

Your *risk profile* refers to how much risk or volatility in the RESP account you can comfortably live with.

In general, riskier investments such as stocks have a higher expected return compared to safer investments such as GICs.

The problem is that stocks are called *risky* for a reason: They can go way up in value and go way down in value as well. If you buy a mutual fund which invests in stocks, you have to be able to handle the fact that the fund value will go down as well as up.

Not every investor has the nerves to own investments that can go down in value. The risk is that if a very conservative investor buys a risky investment, they might sell as soon as the investment goes down in value. To that end, you must decide what kind of investor you are and invest appropriately.

**Here are some sample investor risk profiles:**

**Very conservative**

> This person cannot stand the idea of losing one penny of his investment. Investing in stocks would result in high stress and many nights of lost sleep.

> **Appropriate investments:**
> GICs, high interest savings accounts.

**Conservative, but willing to take some risk**

> This category is basically people who will probably invest in equities, but only a limited amount. This person might have an asset allocation of 70% *safe* investments, such as GICs or short term bonds, and 30% equities such as a stock mutual fund.

104

## Moderate to high risk investor

This investor is comfortable with the risks involved with owning equities and is likely to start off the RESP with 100% equities or close to it. Only later on will they start transferring some of the equities to safer investments as the child gets closer to school age.

## Evel Knievel crazy

This person will want to invest in the riskiest investments allowed in RESP accounts just for the fun of it. In this case, the account beneficiary might have better luck picking the investments, regardless of his or her age.

## Some points to consider

The investment time horizon of the account will change over time. Regardless of your risk profile, the investment choices in the RESP account should get more conservative as the child gets closer to attending post-secondary education.

As William Bernstein wrote in *Four Pillars of Investing*, when deciding on your asset allocation, it is better for one to be too conservative and be able to handle major market drops without selling your equities, than to be selling your equities after big market drops.

## Passive investing vs. active investing

Passive investing refers to buying investment products (either an index fund or ETF) that mimic the performance of a stock or bond index. The return of this type of investment is the same return as the underlying index minus a small management fee. The term *passive* is used because this investment method is not actively managed.

Active investing means investing in mutual funds or individual stocks with the goal of trying to outperform the index. The problem with active investing is that it is not clear that very many people can beat the index over any length of time after accounting for fees. Actively managed mutual funds generally charge high management fees. Even if the actively managed mutual fund does outperform the market, it has to outperform by an amount greater than the management fee for the investor to get any benefit.

In reality, very few mutual funds can beat the market for more than a few years, and it is impossible to predict who those winners will be in advance.

If you are working with an advisor, they will likely want you to buy actively managed funds because the sales commissions are higher. If you go this route, keep an eye on the management fees and ask your advisor to look for less expensive alternatives.

**What does a couple of percentage points matter for mutual fund fees?**

A difference of 1% or 2% in fees per year might not seem that significant, but over time it can add up. If we compare a typical Canadian equity mutual fund with an annual expense of 2.25% to a Canadian index fund with an annual expense of 0.5%, and we assume that the performance of both funds before fees is equal, we might get the following example.

Joe invests $25,000 in the high priced mutual fund. Sue invests $25,000 in the cheaper index fund. If we assume that the underlying stock market index returns 7% per year, how much will each investor have after 15 years?

Joe will have $50,147 and Sue will have $64,296! Yes, Sue will have 28% more money than Joe after 15 years, which is a rather large difference considering they invested in a similar type of investment with a similar amount of risk.

If you want to research the costs on any kind of mutual fund, index fund or ETF, check out GlobeFund.com, which is one of the leaders in Canadian financial information.

**Asset Allocation**

One of the key steps to RESP investing is deciding what your asset allocation should be. "But what is asset allocation?" you ask. Asset allocation is the relative amount of each asset class in your portfolio, and it determines how much risk your portfolio has.

106

For example: One investor might decide to have an asset allocation of 60% stocks and 40% bonds.

Let's take a closer look.

**Asset classes**

An asset class is simply a group of similar investments whose prices tend to **move together**. In other words, their price movements are at least partially correlated.

Asset classes can be defined on a very general level (stocks, bonds, cash) or on a more specific level (Canadian equity, American equity).

The concept of asset classes is important. One of your goals when creating an RESP account should be to practice diversification by using asset classes that are not correlated to each other. That is, you want a portfolio in which not every investment moves the same direction at the same time.

If your assets are not correlated and one of your asset classes performs poorly (such as stocks in 2008), your other asset classes (such as cash) might help make up for it. This works the other way too — if stocks do well, your other asset classes will probably lower the overall return.

**Diversification** lowers the volatility of your portfolio. If you only own stocks, you could have years where you have -40% returns — or +40% returns. If you own a mix of stocks, bonds, and cash, your best and worst years will be a lot less dramatic than with an all-stock portfolio.

**General asset classes include:**
- **Stocks**. This could be individual company stocks or shares of a stock mutual fund, ETF or index fund.
- **Fixed income**. Any type of bond, bond mutual fund or GIC.
- **Cash**. Usually money in a high-interest savings account or GIC.

There are many different asset classes. It is important to be familiar with the general asset classes (stocks, bonds, cash). Later on you

107

can learn about more specific classes if they are applicable to your situation.

You can change the risk level of your RESP account by changing the asset allocation. If your child is very young and you wish to have a fairly risky portfolio, you might want the asset allocation to be 80% equities and 20% GICs. If you are risk adverse and want to make sure the RESP account never loses any money, you might want to invest 100% in GICs.

Many people make the mistake of thinking you need to choose between all risky assets or all safe investments. In reality, you should pick a happy medium. Riskier assets like stocks have a higher expected rate of return. If your investment time horizon is long enough, don't avoid stocks completely just because they're more volatile than fixed income or cash.

**Investment Time Horizon**

The goal is to try to match your time horizon with the risk level of your portfolio.

Your investment time horizon is the length of time until you need to sell your investments. This is an important concept when trying to decide what kind of investment products you should have in your RESP. If the beneficiaries are young and won't be starting school for many years, you might want to own some equities, which are riskier and can go up and down in value, but have a higher expected rate of return. If your children are going to be starting school in the next few years, the money should be invested in very safe investments such as GICs or a high interest savings account, which have a lower expected rate of return.

The combination of your risk profile and time horizon should help you decide which investment products to have in the RESP account.

**Volatility and risk**

The expected return from equities is higher than that of other investments such as cash and bonds. This difference, which is called the *equity premium*, reflects the higher amount of risk assumed when owning stocks. Sometimes investors make the mistake of forgetting

108

that expected returns for equities are only reasonable over the long term (i.e. 20 years or more). Any individual year or even group of years can have a very wide range of returns — both positive and negative. Stock market returns in 2008 are a great example of an extreme negative result.

Long-term bonds can also be fairly volatile if interest rates increase. If interest rates rise, bonds will fall and vice-versa.

On the other end of the spectrum we have cash. The great thing about cash is that although the expected return is very low – roughly 3% at the moment (which doesn't include inflation), at least you don't have to worry about any volatility. If you put $5,000 into a high interest TFSA on January 1, that $5,000 will still be there in June, plus a bit of interest.

**Match the investment to the time horizon**

The lesson to be learnt here is that you have to choose the right type of asset class for your time horizon. If you have a long investment horizon, you can afford the risk of owning some equities. If you have a very short time horizon, you should probably stay in cash. Anything in between should have some combination of risky and guaranteed investments.

The idea behind choosing the proper investment to your time horizon is not to increase your investment return, but rather to **increase the probability** that the required amount of money will be there when you need it.

**Some investment time horizon scenarios**

Here are some sample RESP investment time horizon scenarios. Please keep in mind that there are no agreed upon lengths of time for various time horizons. These are the particular scenarios that I'm planning to use for my children's RESP account. These are based on the fact that I have a high tolerance for risk in my investment portfolios (2008 didn't bother me at all). You need to consider your own situation and/or consult with an investment professional in order to determine the proper asset allocation for your RESP account.

**Long-term horizon – Child is 0 to 6 years old**

This is the time horizon that I am in right now. For my children's RESP account I've invested 100% in equities.

I have:

- 30% Canadian equities
- 30% US equities
- 30% European equities
- 10% Asian equities

This is a very risky portfolio.

Someone who has a more moderate risk profile might choose to only have 50-70% of the account in equities with the remainder in GICs.

Alternatively, someone else might want to have all their investments in GICs or a high interest savings account, which is very conservative.

**Mid-term horizon – Child is 7 to 12 years old**

For this time period, I'm planning to have 60% equities and 40% short term bonds. A more moderate risk profile might have 40% equities and 60% GICs.

**Short-term horizon – Child is 13 years old or older**

At this point, I plan to have 80% bonds and 20% equities and will increase the bond portion in the last couple of years to 100%. I also don't want any currency risk, so the equities will be in Canadian equities. If I have any foreign equities at this point, they will be in currency-neutral versions so that I don't have to worry about currency exchange swings.

Remember that your investment time horizon is always changing. If you have $10,000 invested that you need in 16 years, you might invest in a 60% stocks, 40% bonds mix. After 9 years have elapsed, there will be only seven years remaining in the time horizon, so it would be advisable to increase the bond portion and decrease the stocks portion to lower the risk.

### Rebalancing your RESP account

Rebalancing your portfolio is an important part of investing. Portfolio rebalancing is accomplished by occasionally resetting the proportions of each asset class back to its original percentage. In other words, get the asset allocation back to your original ratio.

The idea behind rebalancing is to maintain a constant risk level in your RESP account. If you intend to have a 50% equities and 50% fixed income asset allocation, and the equities have gone up so much that the ratio is now 55% equities and 45% bonds, your risk level has gone up, and you need to adjust the account to get it back to your original 50/50 ratio.

For example: Assume that Susan has an RESP account for her twin boys that she has been contributing to for several years. She has a desired asset allocation of **60%** equities and **40%** bonds. However, the equity portion of the RESP account has gone down in value over the last three years, and the bond portion has gone up. The asset allocation is now 46% bonds and 54% equities, which is not what she wants.

To rebalance, Susan can do either or both of two methods:

1) Sell some of the bonds and use the proceeds to buy more equities. If she does this correctly, the asset allocation should go back to the original **60/40** ratio.

2) She can change her regular contributions so that all the new money is going into equities. Once the amount of equities in the account is equal to the amount of bonds, she can then change her contributions back to **60% equities and 40% bonds**. This approach is more economical if transaction fees are involved.

There are a couple of reasons to rebalance. First, by selling asset classes that have risen in value and by buying other asset classes that have dropped, you are selling high and buying low. Second, if you don't rebalance, it's possible for your asset allocation (and investment risk) to become radically different from your intended levels.

111

## Investment Diversification

Investment diversification means that an investor should buy investments that are not concentrated in one company, industry, country or even asset class.

You have undoubtedly heard the saying "Don't put all your eggs in one basket". The same principle applies to investing – put your investments into different baskets. If some of the baskets should fail, your losses will still be manageable because of the successful baskets.

It can be tempting to put a large percentage of your RESP into one stock or investment type that you are convinced will do well, but what happens if you are wrong? Your investment could get wiped out! Spreading your investments into different asset classes, industries, countries and even currencies will help guard against a major loss.

## Diversification means different!

If you want to diversify your investments, it is important to ensure you are buying investments which are not correlated with each other – in other words, if you buy three different oil company stocks, you are not really much more diversified than you would be with one oil stock since the factors that affect oil stocks are probably quite similar. If the price of oil drops, that will be a negative factor for all oil companies.

## Here are some ways to diversify your portfolio:

- **Asset classes:** Stocks, bonds and cash are all generally not correlated with each other, so owning some of each will help diversify your investment portfolio.
- **Industry:** If you own stocks either directly or in mutual funds, make sure there is adequate representation from different industries.
- **Country:** Most investors tend to own too much equity in their home country, which reduces their diversification.

It is important to know what you are invested in. If you own mutual funds, find out what the fund holds - ask your advisor if you have one.

112

Index funds and exchange traded funds can be based on any stock index or group of stocks (sub-index) that the fund creator decides on. The problem is that there are a lot of index funds and ETFs that are based on very narrow segments of the economy.

For example: The **RESP Oil Fund** might be an index fund that is intended to reflect the performance of light crude oil. This sounds great for an investor who is interested in oil, but not very suitable for a passive investor who just wants his index funds to be as diversified as possible.

Actively managed mutual funds can invest in whatever the portfolio manager desires within the stated goals of the fund. Don't just look at the fund name and assume you know what is in the fund. Do your research and learn exactly what is in your portfolio.

# Chapter 12 Summary

There are many types of investments eligible for an RESP account. GICs, high interest savings account, individual stocks, mutual funds, exchange traded funds (ETFs) and more.

You can hire an investment professional to manage the RESP or you can do it yourself.

Watch out for the costs of investment products. Try to keep costs to a minimum.

Know what risk level you are comfortable with.

As the child gets closer to post-secondary school age, the RESP account should be invested more conservatively.

# RESP ACCOUNT SETUP CHECKLIST

- ☐ Valid SIN for yourself
- ☐ Valid SIN for each beneficiary
- ☐ Birthdates for each beneficiary
- ☐ Money for an initial contribution or a void cheque to set up a monthly contribution plan
- ☐ Determine how much you are going to contribute and the frequency
- ☐ For a family account, set up the allocations between beneficiaries
- ☐ Decide on a method to pay for contributions: cheques or EFT
- ☐ Choose a financial institution to open the RESP with
- ☐ Determine your risk profile - do you want very safe investments or very risky?  Or something in between?
- ☐ If you are managing your own investments then choose which investment products you wish to invest in

## Once the account is opened

- Check grants received to make sure you are getting the correct amounts
- Monitor contributions and grants to ensure you don't go over grant limits
- Ensure the investment choices are more conservative as the child gets older

## When doing withdrawals

- Have proof of enrolment for beneficiary
- Determine the amount of money to be withdrawn
- Specify or verify the amount of EAP vs. contributions being withdrawn

115

# INDEX

116

## I want feedback!

If you have any kind of comments, questions, complaints or suggestions for improvements regarding this book, I would love to hear from you.

Please send an email to resp@moneysmartsblog.com.

# Acknowledgements

Mike Piper, from The Oblivious Investor, for all his help creating this book. http://www.obliviousinvestor.com/

Kerry Taylor, from Squawk Fox, who is always a big help. http://www.squawkfox.com/

Mr. Cheap, who came up with the idea for this book and encouraged me to write it.